Will Eisner

LAST DAY IN VIETN★M

Diana Schutz ★ editor
Dave Schreiner ★ consulting editor
Cary Grazzini ★ publication design
Mike Richardson ★ publisher

*With thanks to Jim Ottaviani, Ken Lizzi, Michelle Huffman,
and Stephen C. McGeorge, Oregon Military Museum Director,
for their invaluable photo research assistance.*

Published by
Dark Horse Comics, Inc.
10956 SE Main Street
Milwaukie, Oregon 97222

First edition: July 2000
ISBN: 1-56971-437-1

1 2 3 4 5 6 7 8 9 10

PRINTED IN CANADA

DARK HORSE
MAVERICK™

INTRODUCTION

EACH OF THE STORIES in this work were culled from an inventory of encounters with unforgettable people I met during the years I was involved with the military. They are arranged out of personal importance rather than chronology.

Essentially, these are stories about soldiers in wartime who are engaged in a larger combat.

I began military service with the Ordnance Department of the U.S. Army early in the spring of 1942. After my induction I found myself in Aberdeen Proving Grounds, an army camp in Maryland.

The ever-present influence on living in an army post during wartime is the knowledge that you are in transit. The natural tendency is to "hunker down" or settle in and learn the little strategies of survival. A fact of camp life is the importance of quickly coping with the forces that control your destiny.

On our post everyone was concerned about being shipped out. Even though we knew we were there to be trained for service overseas, nearly everyone sought to remain in the comfort of the post. One soldier I knew, an artist, began a portrait of the commanding general which he managed never to finish. That strategy kept him assigned to the post during the general's tenure, which was the entire war.

In the year I was stationed there, I served on the camp newspaper. That position allowed me to witness all sorts of small but weighty dramas in that tight community. It was, I believe, the temporary nature of our residency and the military culture that shaped relationships. Perhaps that is why "A Purple Heart for George," the story related here, left a residue of guilt in many of us. I don't know about the primary actors in that event, which I witnessed, but for me it has never left my mind. I simply cannot forget it.

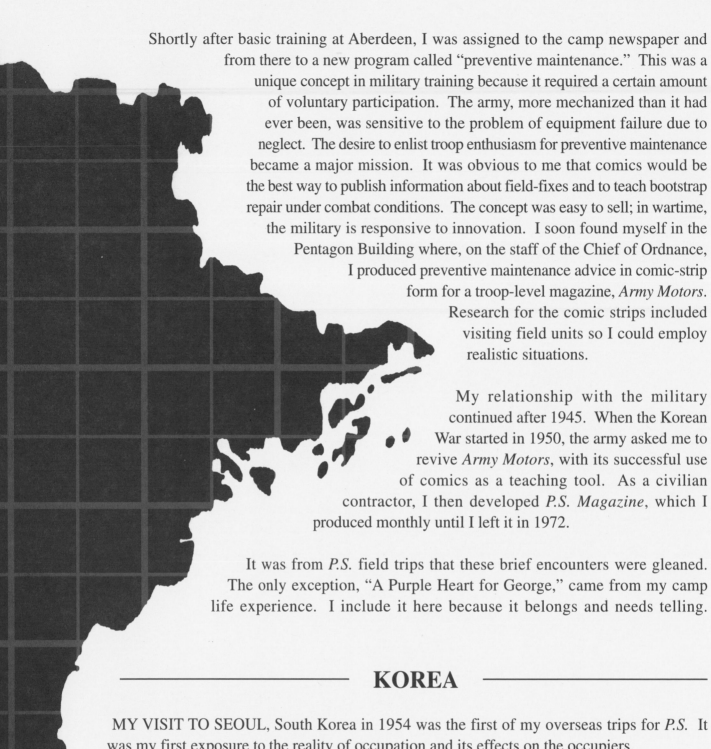

Shortly after basic training at Aberdeen, I was assigned to the camp newspaper and from there to a new program called "preventive maintenance." This was a unique concept in military training because it required a certain amount of voluntary participation. The army, more mechanized than it had ever been, was sensitive to the problem of equipment failure due to neglect. The desire to enlist troop enthusiasm for preventive maintenance became a major mission. It was obvious to me that comics would be the best way to publish information about field-fixes and to teach bootstrap repair under combat conditions. The concept was easy to sell; in wartime, the military is responsive to innovation. I soon found myself in the Pentagon Building where, on the staff of the Chief of Ordnance, I produced preventive maintenance advice in comic-strip form for a troop-level magazine, *Army Motors*. Research for the comic strips included visiting field units so I could employ realistic situations.

My relationship with the military continued after 1945. When the Korean War started in 1950, the army asked me to revive *Army Motors*, with its successful use of comics as a teaching tool. As a civilian contractor, I then developed *P.S. Magazine*, which I produced monthly until I left it in 1972.

It was from *P.S.* field trips that these brief encounters were gleaned. The only exception, "A Purple Heart for George," came from my camp life experience. I include it here because it belongs and needs telling.

KOREA

MY VISIT TO SEOUL, South Korea in 1954 was the first of my overseas trips for *P.S.* It was my first exposure to the reality of occupation and its effects on the occupiers.

On July 23, 1953, the Korean People's Army of North Korea and the United Nations signed a military armistice. They created a demilitarized zone, or DMZ, between North and South Korea. In the south, the allies serving under the U.N. — Turkey, Great Britain, the United States, and Australia — maintained their base camps along the main supply route, or MSR.

Military positions were kept at the ready, and maintenance was a top priority. The U.N. soldiers had to deal with "garrison" duty in a combat posture. In other words, the troops were always supposed to be ready for an attack from the north. The troops moved equipment, repositioned emplacements, and

taught preventive maintenance to the South Koreans.
The experience reinforced my belief that comics can
transcend language barriers. We had great success
with maintenance manuals done in comics or sequential
art form. But all that was merely a background to the
more enduring human encounters.

VIETNAM

I ARRIVED IN VIETNAM during the autumn of 1967. I was based in
Saigon, and my tour was only to last about a month. In the north, the U.S.
Army was struggling to hold onto Khe Sanh, a base just below the DMZ,
running across the narrowest segment of the country.

My job was to visit field units and pick up maintenance stories from automotive
and armament shops. For the most part, I was escorted by the military,
traveling from base to base in a jeep or helicopter.

Saigon was like a stage set. U.S. soldiers dwarfed the native Vietnamese.
Correspondents drank at the sidewalk cafés. Hotels were encased in wire
screens to protect them from the occasional bomb-throwing civilian. The
remnant of a French law office held hundreds of files belonging to plantation
owners who had fled the country a decade before. Because the city was
under military control, it all seemed relatively benign.

It wasn't until the Tet Offensive in January of the following year that Saigon
was partially overrun by the Viet Cong and America became truly aware that it
was losing the war.

During the visits to Korea and Vietnam, I was accompanied by an editor from
P.S. Magazine. To Korea and Japan it was Paul Fitzgerald, and in Vietnam
it was James Kidd. While there, we were often separated, each following a
different story. Neither was actually involved in the incidents narrated here.
Nevertheless their companionship cemented an enduring friendship.

And, finally, my thanks to Dave Schreiner for his thoughtful editing
and his wise advice, which I have so long depended upon, and to
Denis Kitchen for arranging this publication.

Will Eisner

FLORIDA, 2000

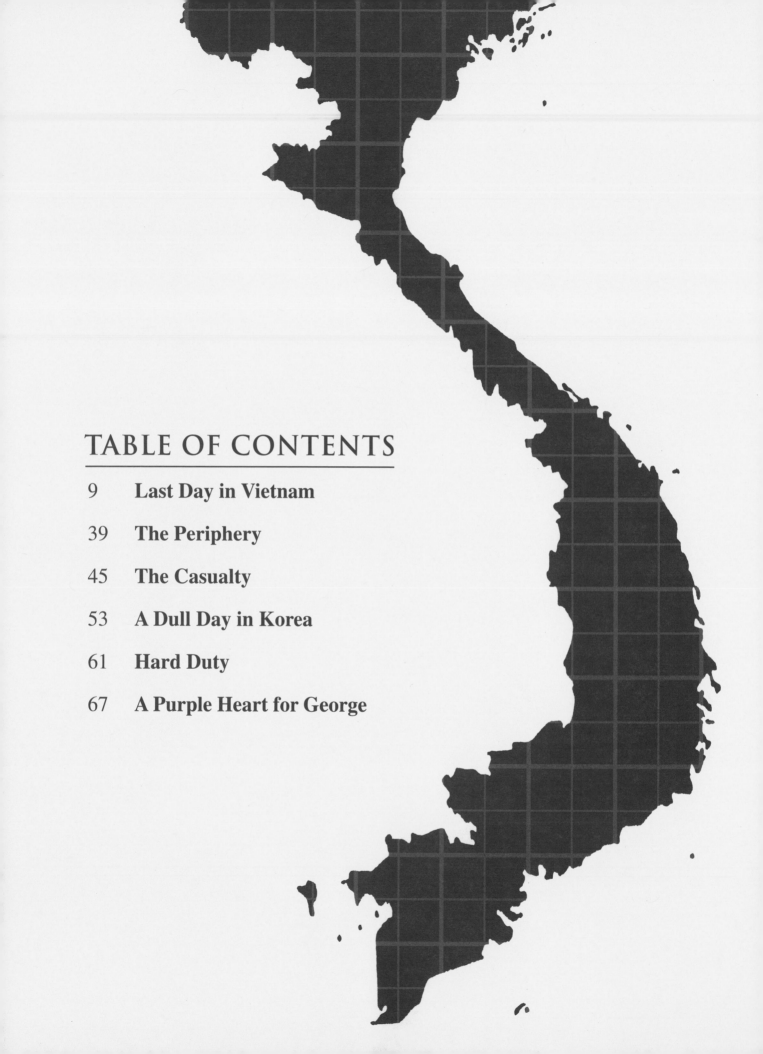

TABLE OF CONTENTS

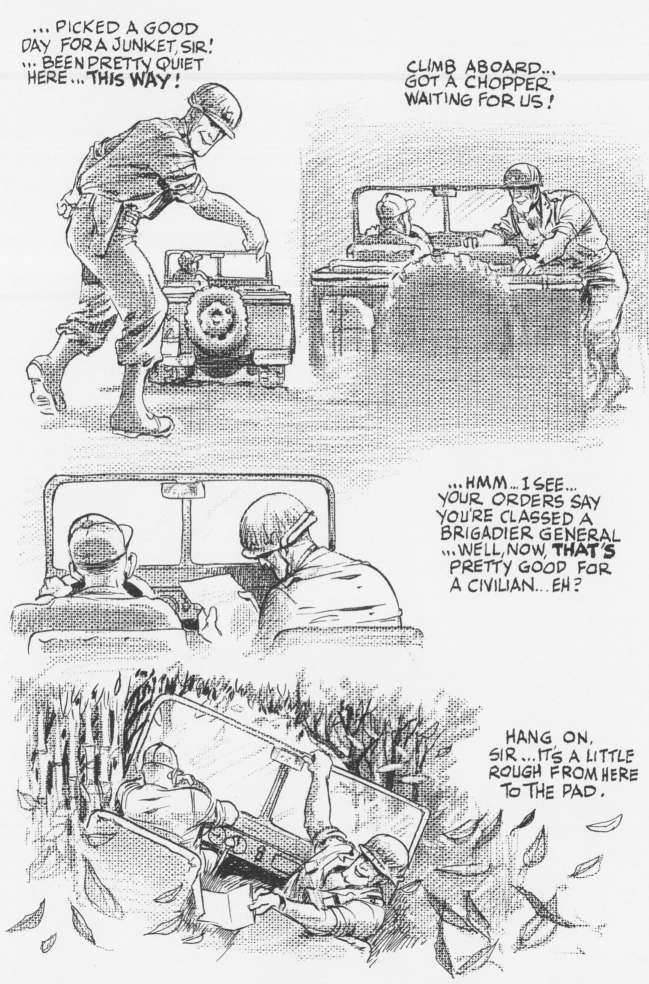

14

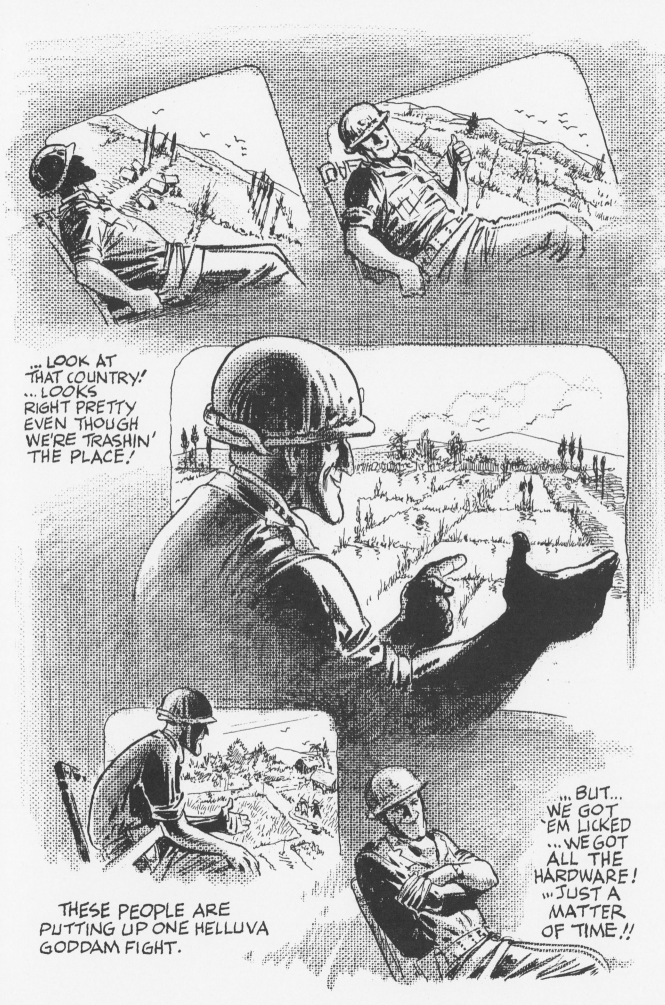

...LOOK AT THAT COUNTRY! ...LOOKS RIGHT PRETTY EVEN THOUGH WE'RE TRASHIN' THE PLACE!

THESE PEOPLE ARE PUTTING UP ONE HELLUVA GODDAM FIGHT.

...BUT... WE GOT 'EM LICKED ...WE GOT ALL THE HARDWARE! ...JUST A MATTER OF TIME!!

18

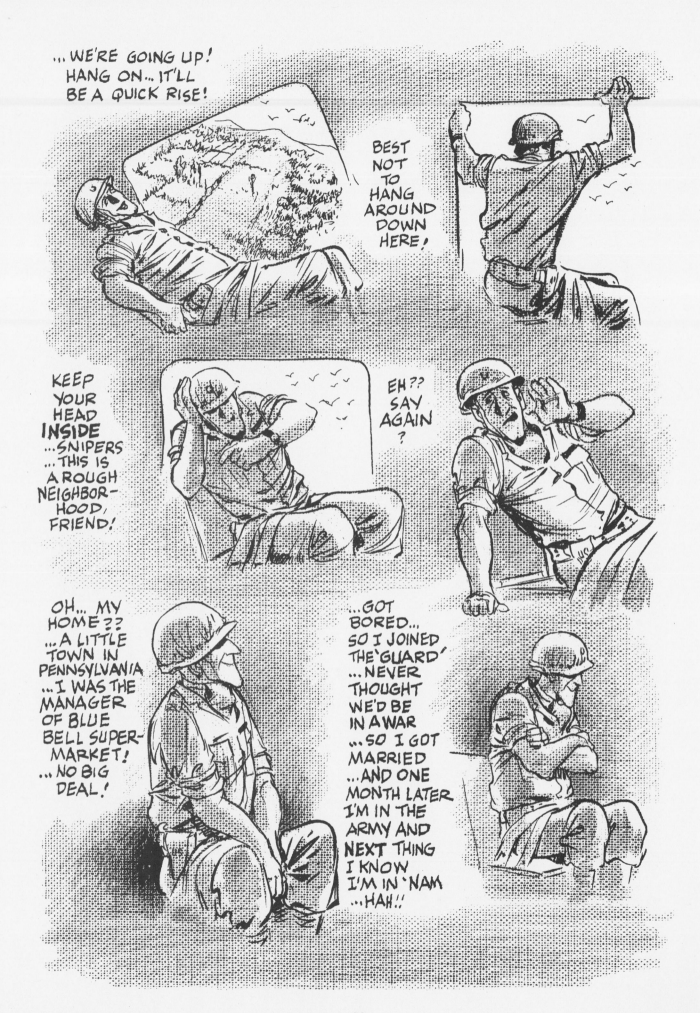

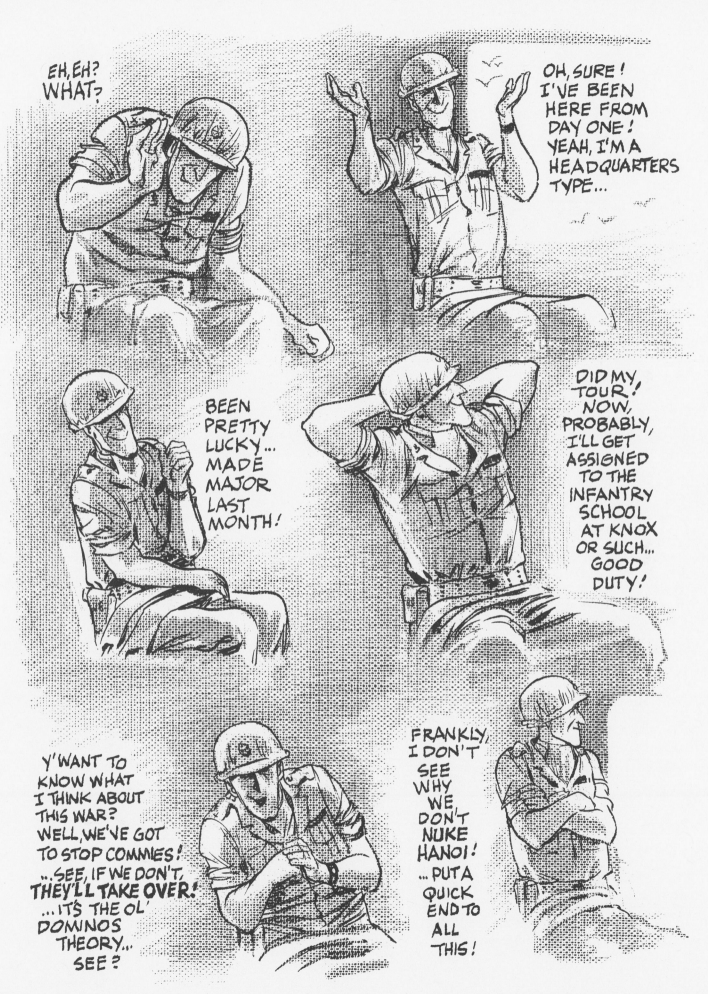

25

26

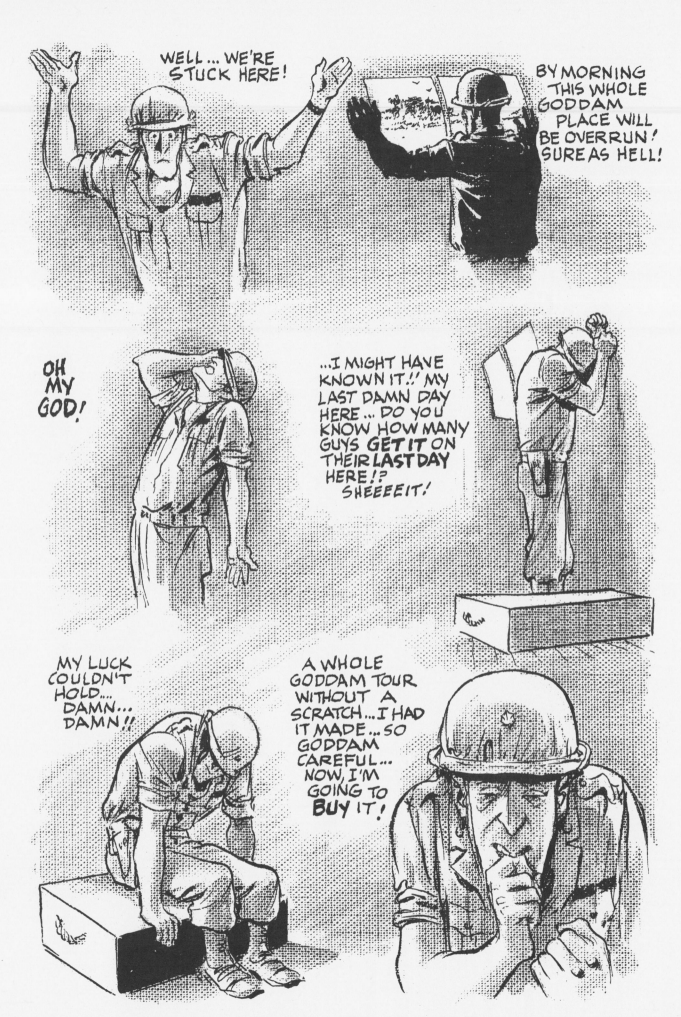

35

GOING
HOME !

THE PERIPHERY

40

41

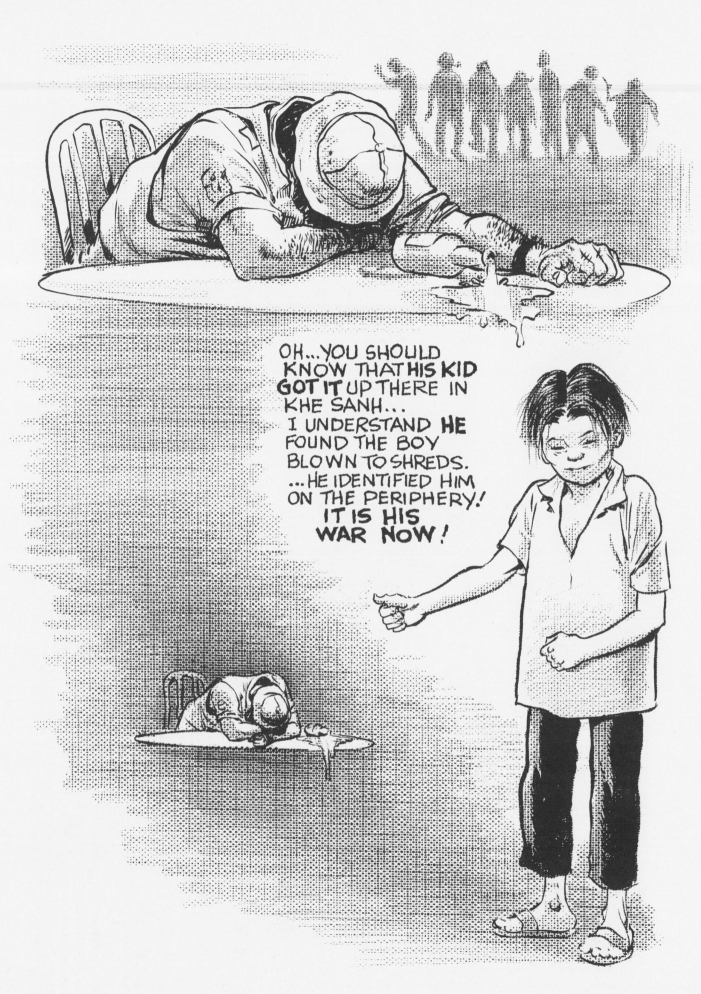

THE CASUALTY

47

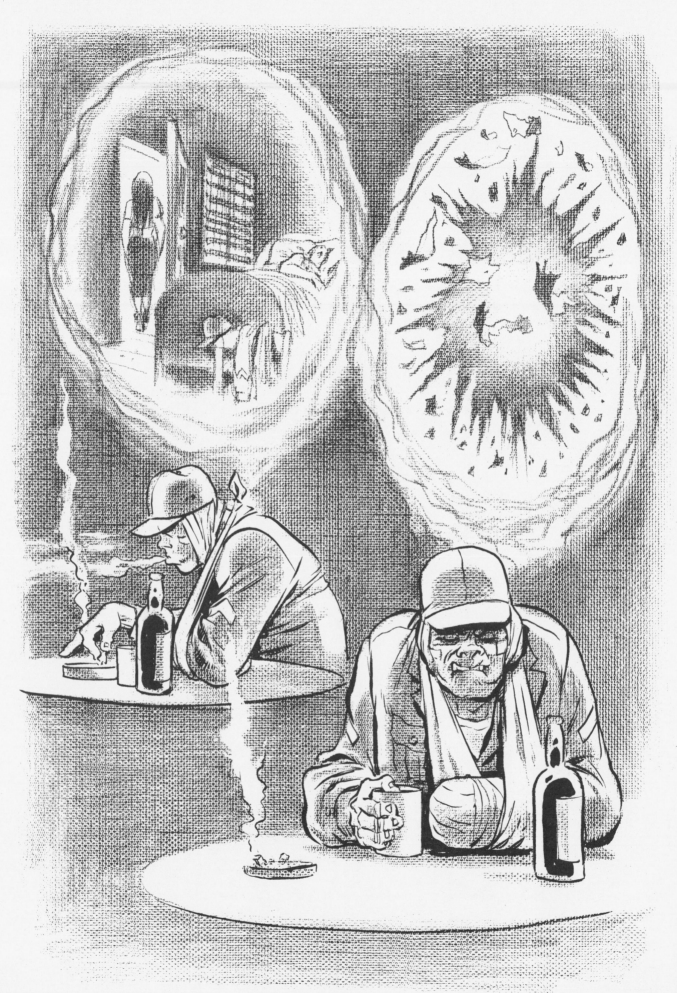

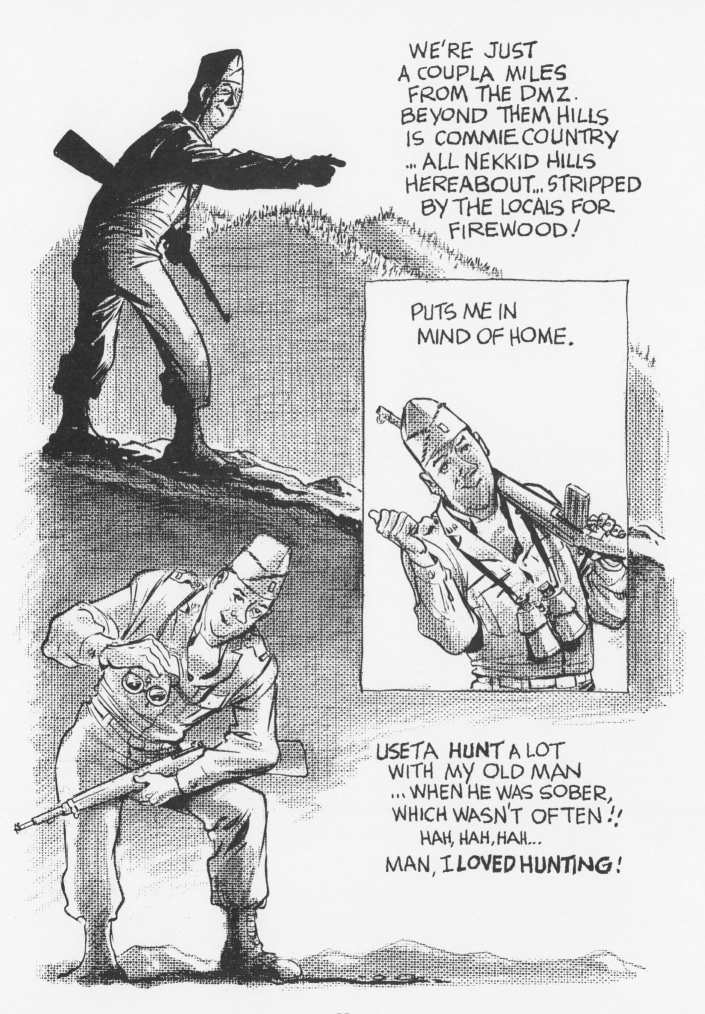

WE'RE JUST A COUPLA MILES FROM THE DMZ. BEYOND THEM HILLS IS COMMIE COUNTRY ... ALL NEKKID HILLS HEREABOUT... STRIPPED BY THE LOCALS FOR FIREWOOD!

PUTS ME IN MIND OF HOME.

USETA **HUNT** A LOT WITH MY OLD MAN ... WHEN HE WAS SOBER, WHICH WASN'T OFTEN!! HAH, HAH, HAH... MAN, I **LOVED** HUNTING!

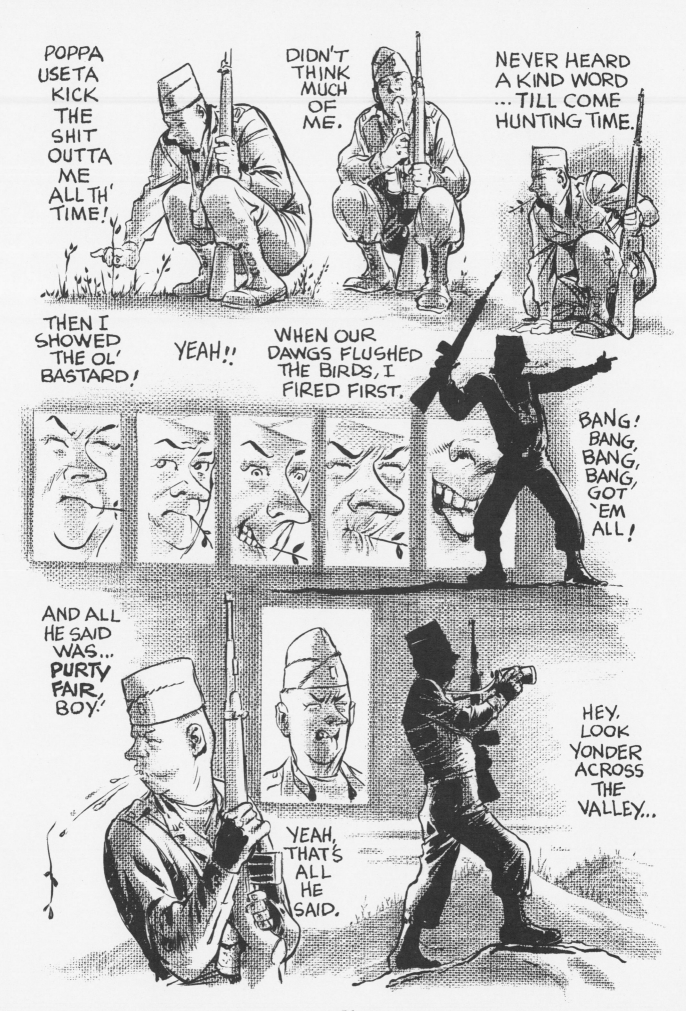

56

58

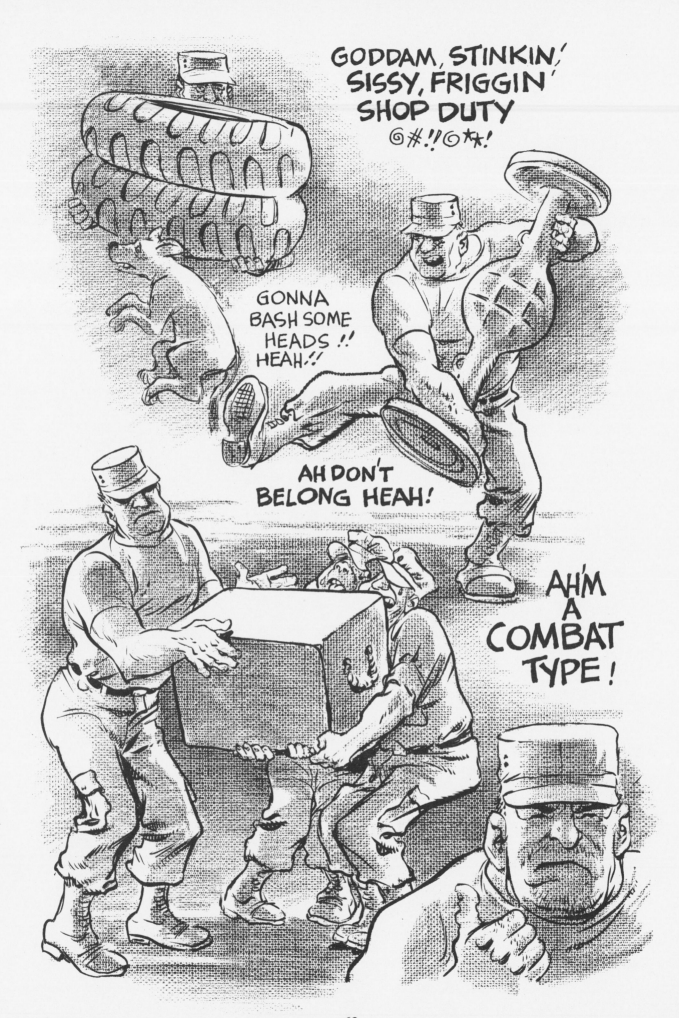

62

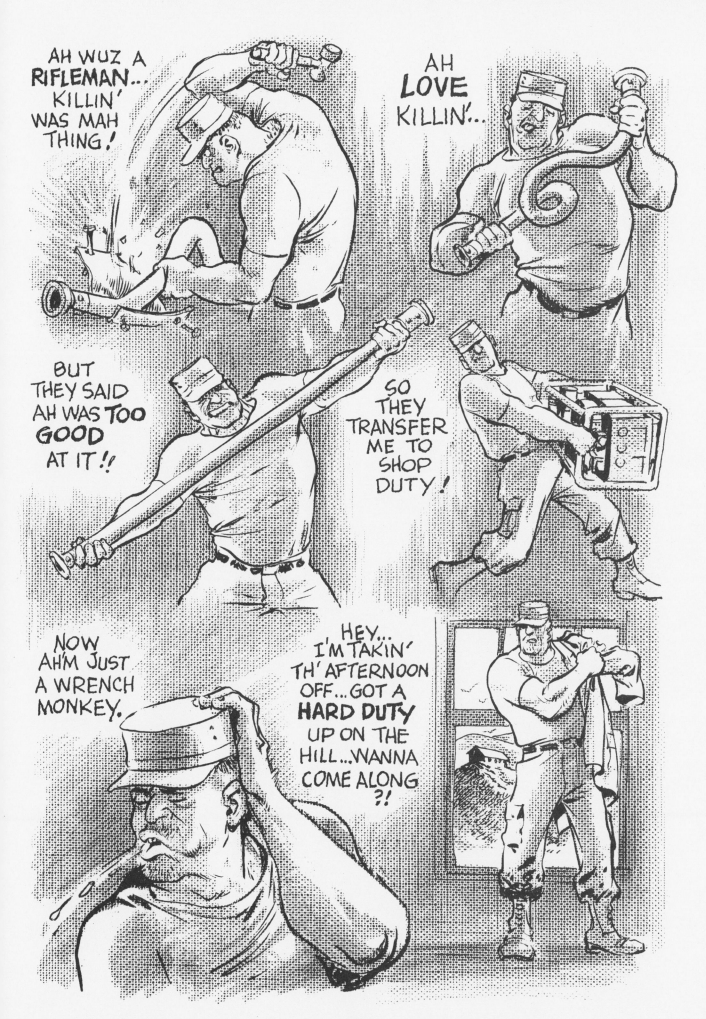

A PURPLE HEART FOR GEORGE

HO! HO!
HO! HO!
YESSIREE,
I'M GONNA
GO!!

71

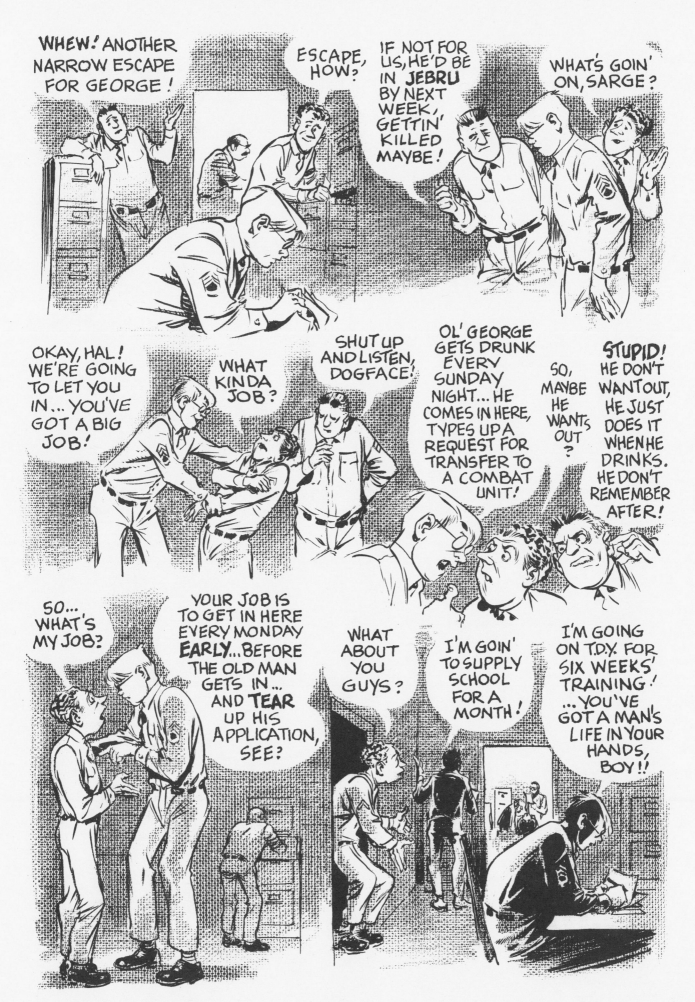

I'M COMING, BENNY!
I'M JOINING YOU, BENNY!
CLICK CLICK CLICK
I hereby apply for transfer to a combat branch, specifically a mine or demolition unit.
CAPT. T. SMITH

The Will Eisner Library

ALL ABOUT P'GELL

In this second volume of *The Spirit Casebook*, the Parisian vixen P'Gell uses her considerable feminine wiles to gain untold wealth while going through more husbands than Elizabeth Taylor! Follow the exploits of *The Spirit*'s most famous femme fatale in sixteen classic stories.

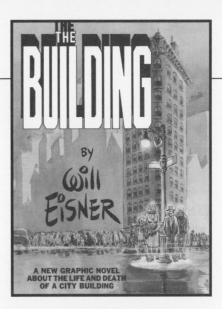

THE BUILDING

Four ghosts appear when a memory-filled building is demolished. *The Building* tells the stories of the ghosts, all connected in some way to the building: Monroe Mensh, whose life is suddenly altered by tragedy; Gilda Green, trapped in an unhappy marriage; P.J. Hammond, who becomes obsessed by the building; and street musician Antonio Tonatti.

LIFE ON ANOTHER PLANET

In this darkly humorous graphic novel, Will Eisner explores the earthly ramifications of first contact with apparent extraterrestrial life, laying bare the vast panorama of human follies and foibles in this wicked mix of science fiction, romance, and social satire.

CITY PEOPLE NOTEBOOK

In this sequel to his *New York* book of graphic essays, Will Eisner examines three facets of city living— time, space, and smell — bringing to his task a lifetime of memories, encounters, and experiences, and sharing them with consummate skill.

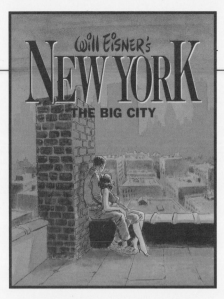

NEW YORK: THE BIG CITY

A treasury of vignettes built around nine elements which, taken together, form Eisner's portrayal of the big city — any city. As a former New Yorker, Eisner's focus inescapably reflects the city of his birth, but the themes inherent in these short pieces transcend the boundaries of any one city and are common to all.

THE SPIRIT ARCHIVES, VOL. 1

In the sixty years since his first appearance, the crimefighting Spirit and his creator Will Eisner have both become legends. This first of a proposed multivolume series of deluxe hardcovers collects the ground-breaking weekly strip from June 2, 1940 to December 29, 1940.

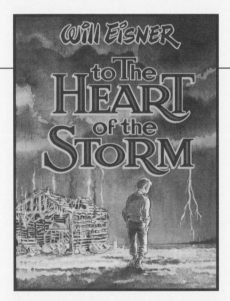

TO THE HEART OF THE STORM

Eisner's most overtly autobiographic work, *To the Heart of the Storm* examines how the anti-Semitism a youth experiences in 1920s and '30s America shapes his personality and his life. It is also a touching family history, told through flashbacks, as a young man rides a troop train to basic training immediately after the entry of the U.S. into WWII.

WILL EISNER READER

This collects seven of the best stories that originally appeared in *Will Eisner's Quarterly* — contemporary tales of poignant reality, imaginative forays into fantasy, ruminations on the human condition, and lighthearted exercises in whimsy.